TAROT

TAROT

PAULA DAY

ELEMENT

Shaftesbury, Dorset • Rockport, Massachusetts • Melbourne, Victoria

© Element Books Limited 1997

First published in Great Britain by
ELEMENT BOOKS LIMITED
Shaftesbury, Dorset SP7 8BP

Published in the USA in 1997 by
ELEMENT BOOKS INC.
PO Box 830, Rockport, MA 01966

Published in Australia in 1997 by
ELEMENT BOOKS LIMITED
and distributed by Penguin Australia Ltd
487 Maroondah Highway, Ringwood, Victoria 3134

Designed and created by
THE BRIDGEWATER BOOK COMPANY

Printed and bound in Singapore

British Library Cataloguing in Publication data available

Library of Congress Cataloging in Publication data available

ISBN: 1 86204 130 X

ELEMENT BOOKS LIMITED
Editorial Director *Julia McCutchen*, Managing Editor *Caro Ness*
Project Editor *Allie West*, Production Director *Roger Lane*
Production *Sarah Golden*

THE BRIDGEWATER BOOK COMPANY
Art Director *Peter Bridgewater*, Designer *Stephen Minns*
Managing Editor *Anne Townley*, Project Editor *Caroline Earle*
Picture Research *Julia Hanson*

Computer illustrations: *Ivan Hissey*, Endpapers: *Sarah Young*

Picture credits:
The Bridgeman Art Library/Christopher Wood Gallery, London – Abraham, Solomon:
Fortune Telling: front cover, 6; Image Bank/Carol Kohen 5; Rex Features 18; U.S. Games Systems Inc., 17.

Illustrations from the IJJ Swiss Tarot deck reproduced by permission of
U.S. Games Systems, Inc., Stamford CT 06902, USA. Copyright © 1974
by U.S. Games System Inc. Further reproduction prohibited.

Illustrations from the Tarot of Marseilles reproduced by permission of
U.S. Games Systems/Carta Mundi. Copyright © 1966 by U.S. Games
System/Carta Mundi. Further reproduction prohibited.

*There are many different views and interpretations of Tarot, some of which may conflict
with each other. This book represents the author's interpretation of the Tarot philosophy,
based on her own information, knowledge, and experience. The book is also a condensed
and simplified form of what can be a complex form of divination.*

*The descriptions and meanings attributed to the Major and Minor Arcana are the author's
own, derived from her knowledge, research, and teachings.*

CONTENTS

INTRODUCTION

Mankind has always been fascinated with the future. The ancient Greeks consulted the oracle at Delphi and the Chinese referred to the Book of Changes, *or* I Ching. *Another age-old form of divination, Tarot has found great popularity in our modern age of uncertainty.*

WHAT IS TAROT?

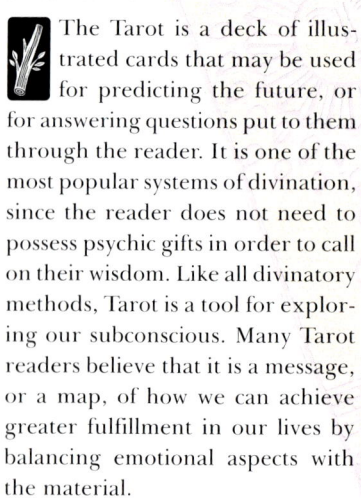

The Tarot is a deck of illustrated cards that may be used for predicting the future, or for answering questions put to them through the reader. It is one of the most popular systems of divination, since the reader does not need to possess psychic gifts in order to call on their wisdom. Like all divinatory methods, Tarot is a tool for exploring our subconscious. Many Tarot readers believe that it is a message, or a map, of how we can achieve greater fulfillment in our lives by balancing emotional aspects with the material.

People who ask questions of the Tarot do so because they cannot see a way out of a problem or a situation. The Tarot cards outline the choices available; this is often a good starting point in helping you solve problems for yourself.

The images portrayed on the Tarot cards are effectively windows through which we can examine our individual lives.

You do not need to possess magic powers or special wisdom to read the Tarot cards. Likewise, Tarot does not depend upon supernatural forces, or psychic energy.

It is possible for anyone to understand and practice Tarot after only a few weeks of study. With experience, however, readers learn to call upon their intuition to make readings more accurate.

A HISTORY OF TAROT

Although the Tarot may have its roots in ancient cultures, it is widely believed to have developed in Renaissance Italy, where a card game, Tarocchi – an ancestor of Bridge – was played.

As a card game, Tarot first appeared in Europe in the 14th century, becoming a popular game for the middle classes and aristocracy. By the middle of the 15th century, an artist named Bonifacio Bembo painted a set of Tarot cards as a wedding present

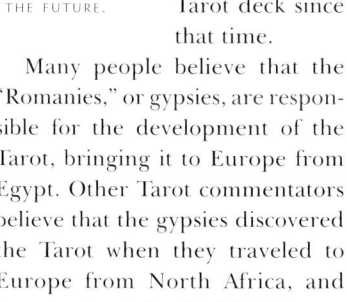

THE TAROT CARDS OF THE PAST HOLD INSIGHT INTO THE PRESENT AND GLIMPSES OF THE FUTURE.

for a union between the Sforza family and the Visconti family of Milan, in Italy.

Incidentally, 150 years earlier, church officials burned to death Maria Visconti, who had been elected the first woman Pope by a group of religious outlaws. To this day, the classic Tarot contains a card entitled "Female Pope." Originally, it would have been a set of picture

cards numbered from 1 to 21 with an extra unnumbered fool card, or joker. It is likely that the Venetians added 56 numeral cards to the Tarot deck, making up the 78-card deck that is still in use in most countries today. The numbered cards were divided into suits, each of which contained a king, queen, knight, and page, along with ten cards without images that were only numbered.

Seventy-four of the original 78-card Tarot deck have survived, and very few changes have been made to the Tarot deck since that time.

Many people believe that the "Romanies," or gypsies, are responsible for the development of the Tarot, bringing it to Europe from Egypt. Other Tarot commentators believe that the gypsies discovered the Tarot when they traveled to Europe from North Africa, and began using it for the highly accurate fortune-telling that has become their trademark today.

Records indicate that in 1459 the Pope and his cardinals used the Tarot as a memory aid and a theological game, that helped to remove some of the pagan stigma attributed to the cards. However, Tarot cards are still known as the "Devil's picture book," a very misleading association since they are purely a tool for divination, not used for Satanic purposes.

The standardization of the Tarot deck came about in the 18th century, when the Tarot of Marseilles became extremely popular. The 18th century also brought the first attempt to link Tarot with ancient pagan esoteric beliefs. In 1781, an archaeologist and esoteric scientist, Antoine Court de Gebelin, published the eighth volume of his work *Le Monde Primitif*, in which he discussed the origins of the Tarot deck and put forward the idea that the cards were a remnant of the ancient Egyptian book of magic, *The Book of Thoth*. Court de Gebelin also suggested that there could be a connection between the cards of the Tarot's Major Arcana and the letters of the Hebrew alphabet.

In 1888, the Hermetic Order of the Golden Dawn was formed. The Order was an esoteric society, founded on the central belief that astrology, divination, numerology, the Cabbala, and ritual magic all formed part of the same system, with the Tarot providing the central key. Well-known members of the order included the poet W. B. Yeats and the writer Bram Stoker. Pamela Colman Smith and A. E. Waite were other notable members, and they were responsible for designing the famous Rider-Waite Tarot deck, and writing a book entitled *The Pictorial Key to the Tarot*, published by Rider (hence the name of the pack).

The renaissance of interest in taking responsibility for our own lives, that characterizes the New Age philosophy, has made the Tarot enormously popular in the 20th century. There are many different Tarot decks to choose from, all varying in complexity of symbolism and in association, from the traditional to the bizarre or surreal.

Various cultures have become connected with the Tarot – including Norse, Tibetan, Mayan, and Aboriginal – and this has only served to enrich the mysterious and vibrant insights of the art.

ABRAHAM SOLOMON'S *FORTUNE TELLING*.
THE "READER" ANALYZES AND INTERPRETS
THE FEATURES OF THE TAROT CARDS
FOR THE "QUERENT."

SETTING THE SCENE

Tarot cards may be used for predicting future events or for answering almost any kind of question put to them by someone familiar with their symbolism. The person interpreting the cards should remember that the interpretation of the official symbolism and meanings of the cards should be adapted to harmonize with the case in question.

HOW TAROT WORKS

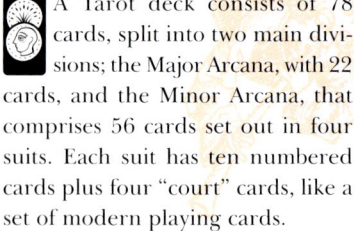 A Tarot deck consists of 78 cards, split into two main divisions; the Major Arcana, with 22 cards, and the Minor Arcana, that comprises 56 cards set out in four suits. Each suit has ten numbered cards plus four "court" cards, like a set of modern playing cards.

The suits have different names: Wands, Rods, or Batons (corresponding to Clubs); Cups (corresponding to Hearts); Swords (corresponding to Spades); and Coins, Pentacles, or Disks (corresponding to Diamonds). The court cards are usually called King, Queen, Knight, and Page.

The 22 cards of the Major Arcana form a sequence of 21 numbered cards, plus one unnumbered card called The Fool (that may be numbered zero in some decks). The Major Arcana is the most symbolic part of the Tarot, depicting unusual scenes and figures with various meanings. More significant than the Minor Arcana cards, these symbolize major changes in your life.

◉ The *"reader" is the owner of the Tarot pack, and the person who will carry out the reading.*

◉ The *"querent" is the person whose cards are being read, and who may have asked for an answer to a particular question.*

FACTORS GOVERNING OUR LIVES

FATE

Inevitable events or circumstances beyond our control in our lives are considered to be our "fate," or "destiny."

FREE WILL

In the West, many of us believe in the concept of free will; in other words, we have the ability to choose the direction our lives take, and we can act accordingly.

EXTERNAL FACTORS

Our lives are also governed by other factors, including our genetic make-up, our personality traits, and our environment.

X

THE WHEEL OF FORTUNE

SYNCHRONICITY

Psychologist and psychoanalyst, Carl Jung (1875–1961) suggested that when coincidence appeared to have a deeper, more significant pattern, it could be called "synchronicity." The theory of synchronicity is applied to Tarot: the patterns in which the cards seem to fall are part of a greater pattern within the "scheme of things." The cards will always be relevant to the querent and the reader.

SYMBOLISM

Tarot cards have images portraying symbols, numbers, and astrological signs, all of which have a deeper symbolism. There are three particular themes that will help you to make sense of the divinatory meanings of the cards, and they are:

⑥ *gender* ⑥ *numbers* ⑥ *elements*

Many decks have deep associations with myths and legends, or with magic and astrology. You will be required to learn the system behind the cards, as well as the principles of reading them, so try to choose a straightforward deck.

In the Minor Arcana, the meaning of each card will be altered by its gender (or sex, which applies to the court cards only), its number (for the pip cards, *see page 36*), and the element (*see page 13*) with which it is associated.

GENDER

It has long been believed that opposing, but complementary, forces at work in the universe govern our daily lives and keep it in balance. These age-old principles (yin and yang in Chinese philosophy) can be considered to be masculine and feminine.

The masculine principle is associated with:

- ⊚ *sun*
- ⊚ *daylight*
- ⊚ *rational thinking*
- ⊚ *extroversion*
- ⊚ *the conscious mind*

Attributes: positive, creative, and active

The feminine principle is associated with:

- ⊚ *the natural world*
- ⊚ *moon*
- ⊚ *night*
- ⊚ *the underworld*
- ⊚ *introversion*
- ⊚ *the unconscious mind*
- ⊚ *feeling and emotions*

Attributes: passive, negative, dark, and destructive

Cards are illustrated with male and female figures, and these qualities should be considered when reading the cards. In the Major Arcana, many cards represent different aspects of either feminine or masculine principles; for example, the card of the Moon has masculine associations. In the Minor Arcana, Wands and Swords represent the masculine (phallic symbols), while Cups and Coins are feminine, with symbols representing the womb.

NUMBERS

 The cards of both the Major and Minor Arcana are numbered. The cards of the Major Arcana are numbered 0–22 and the cards of the Minor Arcana are numbered up to 10 in each suit. Both series of cards are said to depict our struggle through life, from birth to death.

Some Tarot readers choose to read the numbers of the Major Arcana as part of the overall picture, although many readers find this approach too complicated to consider, because the meanings of the cards can be interpreted without analyzing the numerical values.

Generally speaking, the cards numbered from one to 10 are concerned with the beginning of life, maturation, and finding one's place in the world. Cards 11 to 21 are likely to suggest intro-spection, self-analysis, and searching for higher ideals.

In the Minor Arcana, there are 40 num-bered cards, or "pip" cards. Unlike the cards of the Major Arcana that represent spiri-tual matters, the pip cards relate to everyday circumstances and emotions. The meaning of each number is considered in relation to the attributes of the suit to which the card belongs (also determined by the element associated with the suit, *see page 13*).

NUMERICAL VALUES OF THE MAJOR ARCANA	
FOOL	0
MAGICIAN	1
HIGH PRIESTESS	2
EMPRESS	3
EMPEROR	4
POPE	5
LOVERS	6
CHARIOT	7
JUSTICE	8
HERMIT	9
WHEEL OF FORTUNE	10
STRENGTH	11
HANGED MAN	12
DEATH	13
TEMPERANCE	14
DEVIL	15
TOWER	16
STAR	17
MOON	18
SUN	19
JUDGMENT	20
WORLD	21

NUMERICAL SIGNIFICANCE OF THE MINOR ARCANA

ꩰ ACES ~ *Birth*
An ace signifies singularity or unity of several components; individually, each ace represents the four elements of fire, water, air, and earth.

ꩰ TWOS ~ *Opposites*
Two represents a relationship between two entities – for example, loving relationships, or perhaps being torn by opposing loyalty or emotions.

ꩰ THREES ~ *Resolution*
The number three represents creation and the product of a union, such as a child or a book. The number three also represents the connection between opposing forces, and it is associated with fate and divinity.

ꩰ FOURS ~ *Healing*
Four is the number of the material world, representing the four elements and dimensions. Four is associated with nature and order.

ꩰ FIVES ~ *Creation*
Five represents disorder, with the neat and uniform form of four disrupted by the additional one. This number indicates the arrival of difficult times.

ꩰ SIXES ~ *Insight*
Six represents completion, fulfillment, and reward, or justice.

ꩰ SEVENS ~ *Introspection*
Seven is considered to be a lucky number, that represents wisdom and integrity.

ꩰ EIGHTS ~ *Totality*
Eight indicates success, progress, and personal development.

ꩰ NINES ~ *Completion*
Because three multiplied by three equals nine, and three is the creative number, nine is associated with extraordinary creativity. The number nine is also associated with reward.

ꩰ TENS ~ *Conclusion*
Ten represents completion and sufficiency.

ELEMENTS

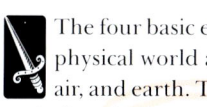 The four basic elements of the physical world are fire, water, air, and earth. These elements are believed to constitute our physical and psychological make-up, and that of the world around us. Each suit of the Minor Arcana has an element associated with it:

⊚ WANDS	*Fire*
⊚ SWORDS	*Air*
⊚ COINS	*Earth*
⊚ CUPS	*Water*

Court cards (*see page 36*) are also associated with the four elements attached to each suit, and because the cards represent people, it is your personality that will be attributed with the qualities of the elements. The specific associations with the elements are:

⊚ KINGS	*Air*
⊚ QUEENS	*Water*
⊚ KNIGHTS	*Fire*
⊚ PAGES	*Earth*

Therefore, a King of Coins would be associated with the characteristics of air and earth. When considering the elements that are associated with each card, it is easy to imagine the qualities that might be attributed. For instance, fire is hot, destructive, spontaneous, and active; water is cool, cleansing, and flowing. Maybe the appearance of an earth element card means that you spend too much time daydreaming and that you need to keep your feet on the ground; maybe an air card is a suggestion that you need some air in your system. The meanings of the Tarot cards can always be individual. Use your intuition to read them.

EARTH

The earth element is associated with:
⊚ THE EMPRESS *Mother, fertility, human understanding, love, marriage, and harmony*
⊚ THE HIEROPHANT *Teacher, guru, stability, wisdom, and tradition*
⊚ THE HERMIT *Critical, analytical, patience, and caution*
⊚ THE DEVIL *Success, materialism, achievements, and wealth*
⊚ THE WORLD *Responsibilities, lessons, and fulfillment*
A heavy emphasis on earth cards means selfishness, a lack of spiritual vision, and a desire to gratify your senses. Lack of earth will result in imbalance, a lack of practicality, and inadequate grounding.

AIR

The air element is associated with:
- ⊙ THE FOOL *Original, adventurous, implusive, and the unexpected*
- ⊙ THE MAGICIAN *Communication, study, learning, and wisdom*
- ⊙ THE LOVERS *Duality, a common cause, and decision-making*
- ⊙ JUSTICE *Balance, cause and effect, and control of fate*
- ⊙ THE STAR *Humanitarian, detached, unemotional, and optimistic*

Too much air makes you out of touch with your feelings. Too little means difficulty in communication.

FIRE

The fire element is associated with:
- ⊙ THE EMPEROR *Leadership, forceful, headstrong, and authority*
- ⊙ STRENGTH *Pride, kinglike behavior, and courage*
- ⊙ TEMPERANCE *Freedom, optimism, and cooperation*
- ⊙ THE TOWER *Energy, action, anger, power, and rebuilding*
- ⊙ THE SUN *Growth, generosity, prosperity, happiness, and purpose*

Fire needs to be controlled because this element can, in excess, be dangerous and destructive. Too much fire can lead to evil, including wars and oppression; too little leaves you feeling listless and results in apathy and depression.

WATER

The water element is associated with:
- ⊙ THE HIGH PRIESTESS *Intuition, telepathy, receptivity, and insight*
- ⊙ THE CHARIOT *Caring, nurturing, and conception*
- ⊙ DEATH *Rebirth, obsessions, sexuality, and change*
- ⊙ THE HANGED MAN *Water, self-sacrificing, and trust*
- ⊙ THE MOON *Sensitive, responsive, and uncertainty*
- ⊙ THE WHEEL OF FORTUNE *Tides, flowing, and abundance*

Too much of the water element eclipses everything around it, and it can lead to over-emotional or, sometimes, irrational behavior. Too little water can mean barren or negative emotions where there is no life or growth.

OTHER SYMBOLS

The following symbols, that appear on different decks, have further meanings, that can be read with the gender, element, and number of your cards:

⊚ CROWN	*High status*
⊚ SCEPTER	*Fertility*
⊚ THRONE	*Strength*
⊚ COLUMNS	*The physical and celestial world*
⊚ KEYS	*Responsibility for unlocking problems*
⊚ PYRAMID	*Transformation, higher reality*
⊚ STARS AND CANOPIES	*Celestial world, higher awareness*
⊚ SQUARE	*Strength*
⊚ TRIANGLE	*Higher spiritual values*
⊚ SPHERE	*Wholeness, completion*
⊚ ARROWS	*Speed, strength, and willpower*
⊚ SNAKE	*Wisdom*
⊚ CORN	*Fertility*
⊚ ROSE	*Love*
⊚ TREES	*Links heaven and earth*
⊚ DOGS	*Loyalty*
⊚ CATS	*Intuition*
⊚ MOUNTAINS	*High achievement*
⊚ BARREN LAND	*Loss or lack of love*

ASTROLOGY AND THE TAROT

Astrological signs also help to define personalities within the Tarot. The signs provide clear traits for each card, and can be read with ordinary star charts. Characteristics of each sign apply to the reading at hand. The cards can be further interpreted by reading the planetary association and applying the influences accordingly.

- ⊚ The Empress ~ *Venus*
- ⊚ The Emperor ~ *Aries*
- ⊚ The Pope ~ *Taurus*
- ⊚ The Lovers ~ *Gemini*
- ⊚ The Chariot ~ *Cancer*
- ⊚ Strength ~ *Leo*
- ⊚ The Hermit ~ *Virgo*
- ⊚ Justice ~ *Libra*
- ⊚ Death ~ *Scorpio*
- ⊚ The Star ~ *Aquarius*
- ⊚ The Moon ~ *Pisces*
- ⊚ The Devil ~ *Capricorn*
- ⊚ The World ~ *Saturn*
- ⊚ The Fool ~ *Uranus*
- ⊚ The Magician ~ *Mercury*
- ⊚ Temperance ~ *Sagittarius*
- ⊚ The Tower ~ *Mars*
- ⊚ The Sun ~ *Sun*
- ⊚ The High Priestess ~ *Moon*
- ⊚ The Hanged Man ~ *Neptune*
- ⊚ The Wheel of Fortune ~ *Jupiter*
- ⊚ Judgment ~ *Pluto*

TECHNIQUES

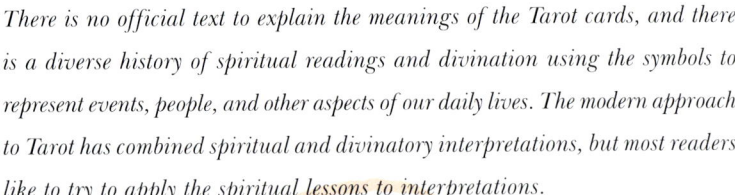

There is no official text to explain the meanings of the Tarot cards, and there is a diverse history of spiritual readings and divination using the symbols to represent events, people, and other aspects of our daily lives. The modern approach to Tarot has combined spiritual and divinatory interpretations, but most readers like to try to apply the spiritual lessons to interpretations.

A TAROT READING

Readings rely as much on your own personal intuition as they do on the features of the Tarot cards themselves. It involves bringing intuitive feelings and unconscious impressions into the conscious part of the mind, where it can sometimes provide helpful advice about the future. In order to call up these unconscious impressions, it is essential that the mind is quiet and uncluttered. Some people find it useful to meditate before a reading, others like to invoke a sense of ritual – offering a small prayer, perhaps burning some incense, or lighting candles.

When doing a reading, remember that it is not essential to have memorized the face values of each of the cards and their interpretations. The best way to get a successful reading is to rely on your feelings; analyze the features of the cards that jump out at you. For example, if you turn over The Fool, you may be struck by the backpack he is carrying, or by the dog on the card. Ask yourself what these features mean to you, and base your reading on your instincts rather than a strict, by-the-book interpretation. It might mean that your querent is planning a trip, or that they have a good, loyal friend (represented by the dog).

THE CARDS

It is generally believed that the Tarot reader should choose a deck that he or she finds attractive, or is drawn to. Alternatively, some readers suggest that decks should not be purchased by the user, but should be given as a gift. Whatever the case, it is essential that you feel comfortable with the deck you are reading from. It is also advised that you do not use someone else's cards – everyone has a different psychic "aura," and cards owned and used by one person will inevitably have that aura, or "energy," stamped upon them.

SYMBOLS, NUMBERS, AND SIGNS MAKE UP THE COLORFUL, LIVELY IMAGES OF THE TAROT PACK.

Many readers believe that the cards should be wrapped in a piece of black or purple silk, and placed in a box, so that their energy does not weaken. You should not allow anyone other than the querent to touch your cards, and even then they ·may only shuffle them and make a selection.

You should always do a reading in a quiet room, and avoid having distractions of any sort. Both the reader and the querent should be able to concentrate fully; the result will be diminished if they are unable to do so.

When laying out the cards in a spread, you may want to place them on a cloth made of black silk, or some other dark material. This is intended to enhance the energy of the Tarot cards, and make the reading more accurate.

READING THE CARDS

Divining with Tarot involves reading the cards. Some people do this by turning cards over at random, and using their intuition to see what strikes them as most relevant. The cards are usually laid down in specific patterns, or what are known as "spreads."

Each position within that spread has its own meaning, and you must take into consideration its position, and the features and associations of the card itself. The accuracy of a reading lies in the reader's ability to interpret and communicate the message depicted in the cards, and their various combinations, and the querent's response to the images.

A reading reveals current events in a person's life or events that should be occurring. The reading will raise relevant issues that need

SPREADING OUT THE CARDS, THE READER USES INTUITION, INTERPRETATION, AND THE QUERENT'S RESPONSES.

to be looked at by the querent rather than accurately pin-pointing what is going on.

The procedure is as follows:

⊚ *The reader chooses a spread that they are comfortable with. You can use the same spread each time or base your choice on intuition, that will change with each querent. Some readers do not use spreads, but simply lay the cards out on a cloth and read them as they are turned up.*

⊚ *Some forms of Tarot suggest that a Significator card be chosen. This is a card that represents the person seeking a* reading, or the situation about which the advice is being sought. (See the next section for details on how to choose the Significator according to physical appearance.) If the Significator card is chosen to represent a situation, you will use your best judgment; a query about getting a new job might require the Wheel of Fortune. For a query involving a legal matter, you might choose the Justice card.

⊚ *The querent mixes the cards, concentrating and gently breathing onto the cards as he or she does so, and then separate the pack into three piles. Alternatively, the querent may choose to fan out the cards, selecting the correct number required for the reading, and then handing them to the reader, who will lay them into a spread.*

⊚ *The reader lays out the cards in the chosen spread.*

⊚ *The cards are turned up, and the reader assesses the overall picture of the spread. Is there a predominance of one suit? Are there any numbers that appear more often? If, for example, there are a large number of Cups, then the main theme suggests love and relationships. A predominance of Wands suggests that a job or worklife is likely to be important. Swords suggest conflict, and Coins suggest practical matters. A large number of cards from the Major Arcana is a sign of change, out of control of the querent.*

⦿ *The reader will then assess the individual cards, one by one.*

⦿ *The reader may ask the querent for their response to the card. Some readers find the contributions of the querent an invaluable tool in interpreting the cards and their message.*

THE SIGNIFICATOR

KING OF WANDS
Fair-haired or auburn-haired man, over 40 years of age with blue eyes, and a fair complexion.

QUEEN OF WANDS
Fair-haired or auburn-haired woman, over 40 years of age with blue eyes, and a fair complexion.

KNIGHT OF WANDS
Fair-haired or auburn-haired man, under 40 years of age with blue eyes, and a fair complexion.

PAGE OF WANDS
Fair-haired or auburn-haired woman, under 40 years of age with blue eyes, and a fair complexion.

KING OF CUPS
Man over 40 years of age, with light brown hair, and gray or blue eyes.

QUEEN OF CUPS
Woman over 40 years of age, with light brown hair, and gray or blue eyes.

KNIGHT OF CUPS
Man or boy under 40 years of age, with light brown hair, and gray or blue eyes.

PAGE OF CUPS
Woman or girl under 40 years of age, with light brown hair, and gray or blue eyes.

KING OF SWORDS
Man over 40 years of age, with dark hair and green or gray eyes, and a dull complexion.

QUEEN OF SWORDS
Woman over 40 years of age, with dark hair and green or gray eyes, and a dull complexion.

KNIGHT OF SWORDS
Man under 40 years of age, with dark hair and green or gray eyes, and a dull complexion.

PAGE OF SWORDS
Woman under 40 years of age, with dark hair and green or gray eyes, and a dull complexion.

KING OF COINS
Man over 40 years of age, with dark skin, hair, and eyes.

QUEEN OF COINS

Woman over 40 years of age, with dark skin, hair, and eyes.

KNIGHT OF COINS

Man under 40 years of age, with dark skin, hair, and eyes.

PAGE OF COINS

Woman under 40 years of age, with dark skin, hair, and eyes.

ASKING A QUESTION

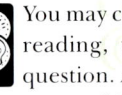 You may choose to do a simple reading, with one card per question. Ask your querent to choose a card from the deck while thinking of a question. The card picked can be read as the answer to their chosen question.

You may choose to do a more complex reading with more cards; there is not any fixed number of cards. Set out the number of cards that feels right to you.

When the querent asks a question during the course of a reading, you can read the cards in front of you as the answer. Another question can be answered by the same cards, with different aspects, symbols, and associations working to create a different answer to the question. Keep the same spread, but use the cards in different ways for each question.

SPREADS

 There are a huge number of spreads within which your reading can be done. Here, we'll discuss two:

◉ *The Three-Card spread*
◉ *The Celtic Cross spread*

THE THREE-CARD SPREAD

PAST   PRESENT   FUTURE

The Three-Card spread is very easy, useful for a beginner, or when you don't have much time. Take time to assess the variables wherever possible, and remember to use your intuition when reading the cards, rather than relying on their straight face value.

◉ *Ask your querent to choose three cards; if you are doing the Tarot reading for yourself, choose the top three cards from the deck.*
◉ *Lay the cards in any order face down in front of you.*

 Place the cards to the left, center, and then right.

 The card to your left refers to the past.

 The card in the center refers to the present.

 The card to your right represents the future.

The card in the past position will represent any prior influences, or previous events, that may have an impact on the present situation. Read the card in the past position in relation to the problem or query at hand.

The card in the present position should represent the answer to the question that the querent asked of the Tarot.

The card in the future position represents events yet to happen, taking into consideration how the present may influence the future.

Look out for things that may connect the cards.

An example:

 The past   *Seven of Wands*

 The present   *Four of Coins*

 The future   *Ace of Coins*

READING

The querent may have had problems recently because another party did not do their job properly, or because they have let problems build up. They may be anxious over money matters or it appears that they may be offered a new job with better financial prospects.

REVERSE MEANINGS

A reverse meaning is attributed to a card when it appears upside down in a spread. Reverse meanings are normally negative aspects of upright meanings, or an absence of the qualities likened to the upright meaning. Some Tarot readers prefer to read the cards as if they were all upright.

THE CELTIC CROSS

 The simplest spread, and probably the most popular, is the Celtic Cross spread. Each position has a particular meaning, representing:

1. the present
2. obstacles
3. past influences
4. future influences
5. past events
6. future events
7. personality
8. home life
9. hopes and fears
10. outcome

It can also be read in response to a question, giving the various positions the following meanings:

1. the central issue
2. obstacles or crossing influence
3. past influences
4. recent developments
5. possible developments
6. approaching influence
7. self
8. others (other related conditions; home life or environmental factors, etc.)
9. hopes and fears
10. outcome (the response to the query)

THE CELTIC CROSS

1. The seven of cups
2. The eight of swords
3. The four of swords
4. The five of cups
5. The five of swords
6. The four of cups
7. Temperance
8. The two of cups
9. The Devil
10. The Sun

READING

 Based on this spread, the querent's general situation shows great frustration and confusion. They have lost their direction in life. It may be advisable to spend time alone, contemplating what they want most out of life, perhaps a break or vacation.

The past events imply hurt and disillusionment in previous relationships, with both lovers and friends. These feelings prevent them from forming new attachments.

The future suggests the querent will become associated with someone whom they would not normally be attracted to – not their "type." If they accept this person's personality, it is likely to lead to a new, and mutually beneficial relationship.

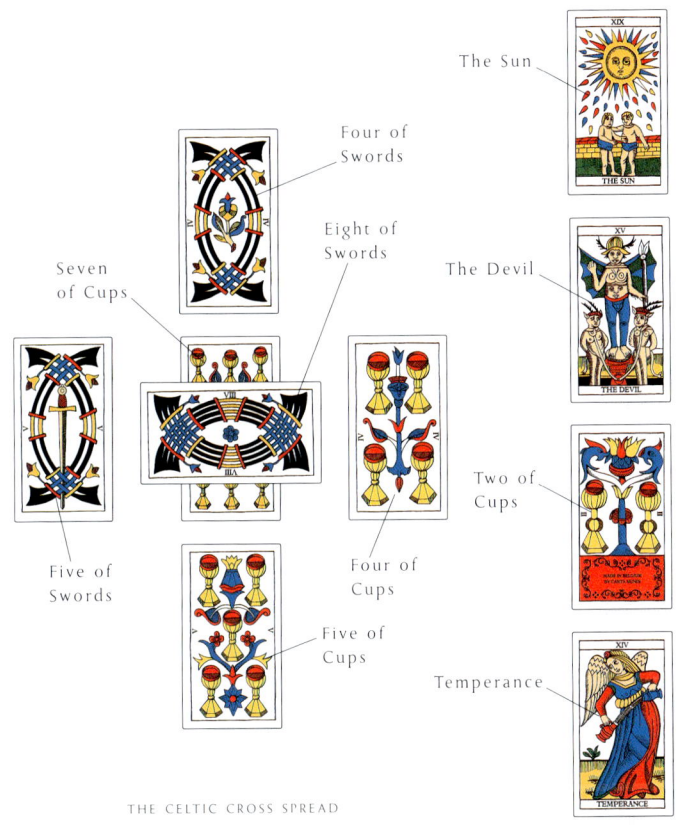

The Sun

Four of
Swords

Eight of
Swords

The Devil

Seven
of Cups

Five of
Swords

Four of
Cups

Two of
Cups

Five of
Cups

Temperance

THE CELTIC CROSS SPREAD

It is crucial the querent learns from their past problems and mistakes, and does not perpetuate negative aspects of their personality. Only then can they let go of the past and embrace the happiness and achievement that await them.

Do not be alarmed if a reading seems to be showing the opposite to what is occurring at present in your querent's life. It may be showing blockages and barriers that are preventing their full potential from being realized.

THE MAJOR ARCANA

The 22 cards of the Major Arcana represent the various stages of our lives on earth from birth, through maturation, to death. The symbolism of this passage begins with the naïve Fool, and culminates in the Judgment.

THE CARDS

The Major Arcana express the journey of our soul; from the innocence of childhood, through various trials, on to maturity, old age, death, and then a spiritual consummation. Some readers believe that the cards represent archetypes, or symbolic figures that appear in the mythology and religion of cultures across the world, and that reappear in dreams of people who have never really heard of them. This theory is based on the belief that these universal figures appear to all of us because they are meaningful to mankind. For example, the Empress can be called the Universal Mother; the Hermit can be seen as a wise old man.

The Major Arcana (from *arcanum*, or "mysterious wisdom known only to the initiate") are also known as Tarot trumps. Many readers choose only to read the Major Arcana; this is possible because of the great symbolism of the cards. They involve the more spiritual, profound level of existence, as opposed to the minutiae of day-to-day living.

Many people are superstitious about the use of Tarot, and even today there is an overwhelming belief that they are an evil or bad influence. Take this into account before doing a reading for others. Cards such as Death or the Devil can be very frightening for the querent, and it is up to you as the querent's interpreter to create a relaxing atmosphere and set their minds at ease before the reading.

THE FOOL

0

Element: AIR
Planet: URANUS

THE MAGICIAN

1

Element: AIR
Planet: MERCURY

Description: The Fool is a young man in a colorful costume with worldly possessions tied in a cloth at the end of a stick. He carries a walking stick in his right hand and has a dog with him that has torn the cloth of his breeches. He strides toward adventure.

Key words: Spontaneity, trust, risk-taking.

Meaning:

◉ *A new perception of the world.*

◉ *Be an individual.*

◉ *Strive for adventure and for your dreams.*

◉ *Develop new skills, new techniques, or new abilities.*

Bullet meaning: A new phase of life is opening up, with many opportunities for change.

Reverse meaning: Fools rush in where angels fear to tread. A child-like view of the world; not accepting responsibilities.

Description: The Magician stands behind a table wearing a wide-brimmed hat. On the table are various conjuror's implements such as cups, balls, and dice. In his left hand he holds a wand and a small ball in his right.

Key words: Skill and confidence, communication.

Meaning:

◉ *Wisdom through improved communication.*

◉ *This card means you will use your knowledge to influence the minds of others.*

◉ *This card symbolizes learning, teaching, and intellectual ability and knowledge.*

Bullet meaning: Improve your communication. You should try to use your skills to spread your message.

Reverse meaning: Trickery, lies, delay.

THE HIGH PRIESTESS

2

Element: NONE
Planet: MOON

THE EMPRESS

3

Element: NONE
Planet: VENUS

Description: The High Priestess is seated, wearing long, flowing robes and a triple crown, with an open book on her knees. In other decks she is also called the Female Pope.

Key words: Intuition, dreams, and knowledge.

Meaning:

◎ *Intuitive knowledge and common sense.*

◎ *Hidden things may be revealed.*

◎ *Look for the answer to your question in your own past experience.*

◎ *We will be able to remold our lives by using our subconscious minds effectively.*

Bullet meaning: Use your intuition and subconscious mind for inspiration.

Reverse meaning: Superstition and nonsense, emotional insecurity and lack of foresight.

Description: The Empress is represented by a fair-haired woman who sits on a throne. In her right hand she holds a protective shield with an eagle symbol upon it and a scepter in her left hand.

Key words: Security, motherhood, and well-being.

Meaning:

◎ *Natural creativity, fruitfulness, and fertility are important. You have the ability to create.*

◎ *Now is the time to locate your creative vein and exploit it.*

◎ *If you are a woman, the card signifies fertility so perhaps it is a good time to have a baby.*

Bullet meaning: Use your own creativity. Act on creative or fecund impulses.

Reverse meaning: Stifling jealousy, maternal tyranny.

THE EMPEROR

4

Element: FIRE
Sign: ARIES

THE HIEROPHANT

5

Element: EARTH
Sign: TAURUS

Description: The throned Emperor sits facing to the right and holds a scepter that symbolizes power and mercy. At his feet is a shield bearing an eagle – like that of the Empress.
Key words: Authority, responsibility, and promotion.
Meaning:

◎ *This card represents a dynamic strength of personality and great leadership qualities.*

◎ *You should be independent, and challenge anything you are unhappy with.*

◎ *Be assertive; use your own judgment to take control of your life and realize your ambitions.*

Bullet meaning: A wish for independence.
Reverse meaning: Weakening of power. Passion over intellect. Instinct over reason.

Description: A Pope is seated in between two pillars holding a papal scepter. He blesses two monks kneeling before him with his right hand. In other decks he is also known as the Hierophant.
Key words: Professional advice, learning, and teaching.
Meaning:

◎ *This card may symbolize spiritual or religious authority and teaching.*

◎ *You may have to make compromises to continue in your direction.*

◎ *This is the point in your life where you should accept your lot; make this the turning point and carry on in the same direction from here.*

◎ *The Hierophant marks ritual and initiation, perhaps marriage, or the progression from innocence to maturity.*

Bullet meaning: An influential teacher entering your life.
Reverse meaning: Dogmatic, brainwashing, and conformist views.

THE LOVERS

6

Element: AIR
Sign: GEMINI

THE CHARIOT

7

Element: WATER
Sign: CANCER

Description: From a blazing sun Cupid aims his arrow at a young man dressed in colourful robes who is torn between two women.

Meaning:

⊚ *This card symbolizes harmony, the connection of opposites, and emotional intensity.*

⊚ *You must regard any upsets in your relationship as a challenge to be overcome.*

⊚ *There is a focus on love, attraction, relationships, and change.*

⊚ *Old bonds may still be strong.*

Bullet meaning: Intensity. Consider choice in relationships.This card signifies that a decision must be made.

Reverse meaning: Folly, unrequited love, and unrealistic attraction.

Description: A king carrying a scepter in his right hand drives a magnificent chariot pulled by two horses; these symbolize good and evil. The two horses are pulling in divergent directions.

Key words: Willpower, ambition.

Meaning:

⊚ *This card symbolizes unstable forces of change.*

⊚ *You may be ascending to higher understanding.*

⊚ *The card represents change, providence, and problems overcome.*

⊚ *Take control of a situation while remembering the importance of compromise.*

Bullet meaning: Once you have decided your chosen path, stick with your direction; don't change your horses halfway.

Reverse meaning: Defeat, setbacks, obstacles and struggle.

JUSTICE

8

Element: AIR
Sign: LIBRA

THE HERMIT

9

Element: EARTH
Sign: VIRGO

Description: A robed figure with a golden crown holds an upheld sword in one hand and a pair of scales in another.

Key words: Justice, reason, legal matters, balance.

Meaning:

⊚ *Reason and justice will prevail.*

⊚ *Certain aspects of your life are unbalanced; you must try to make things more harmonious.*

⊚ *You may be involved in a legal dispute, but the outcome will be just and fair.*

⊚ *Before making a decision, make sure you have taken everything into consideration.*

Bullet meaning: Redress the balance in your life.

Reverse meaning: Injustice, an unfair outcome, bias, bigotry, and narrow-mindedness.

Description: A lone elderly man carries a staff in his left hand, his way guided by his lamp.

Key words: Independence, solitariness, and aloneness.

Meaning:

⊚ *Meditation is one way to achieve liberation.*

⊚ *An inner search will aid personal growth in self-development.*

⊚ *This card symbolizes an important situation in your life – perhaps you are about to progress to a new stage.*

⊚ *You need to remove any difficulties from the current situation before moving forward.*

⊚ *This card represents wisdom, solitude, and discrimination. You will be self-aware and self-knowing.*

Bullet meaning: Look before you leap; act cautiously.

Reverse meaning: Loneliness, feelings of exclusion.

WHEEL OF FORTUNE

10

Element: NONE
Planet: JUPITER

STRENGTH

11

Element: AIR
Sign: LIBRA

Description: A wheel of fortune, with a sphinx at the top symbolizing destiny. On the right side a dog tries to climb the wheel, while on the left a monkey descends.

Meaning:

ⓖ *Keep the karmic laws and success will abound.*

ⓖ *Chance events or occurrences may be beyond your control, but take advantage of what unexpected opportunities fate can offer.*

ⓖ *You must let things run their natural course – for the key to success is being adaptable.*

ⓖ *Changes that occur will be positive.*

Bullet meaning: Abundance, overindulgence. Chance, good luck, fate.

Reverse meaning: Misfortune, bad luck.

Description: A woman dressed in long robes wearing a broad brimmed hat easily opens the jaws of a lion.

Key words: Moral strength, control of your emotions.

Meaning:

ⓖ *This card symbolizes self-discipline, so make use of reason rather than living by emotions alone.*

ⓖ *You will need to have courage in order to succeed, and you will be successful as a leader if you have faith in yourself.*

ⓖ *This card represents power, success, balance, and energy.*

ⓖ *Have faith in yourself.*

Bullet meaning: Use your head, not your heart.

Reverse meaning: Helplessness and inhibition. Inability to cope and negative feelings.

Note: In some decks Strength is 8 and Justice is 11.

THE HANGED MAN

12

Element: WATER
Planet: NEPTUNE

DEATH

13

Element: WATER
Sign: SCORPIO

Description: A man hangs upside down from a tree. His arms are tied behind him and he is secured by one foot, and his legs are crossed in the shape of a figure four.

Key words: Sacrifice, dedication.

Meaning:

⊙ *Wisdom comes from sacrifice, and the secrets of divination with circumspection.*

⊙ *This card represents wisdom, circumspection, trials, sacrifice, prophecy, and change, and reveals that you are experiencing an awakening of your intuitive powers.*

⊙ *Your life will be enriched by self-knowledge.*

⊙ *There is a desire for dedication.*

Bullet meaning: Time is needed for contemplation; you are dedicated to a cause or belief.

Reverse meaning: Dissatisfaction, apathy. To be selfish, looking at the world from the wrong way.

Description: Death is symbolized here by a skeleton that walks with a scythe in his hand across a gruesome field of heads, hands and bones. In other decks he may be a figure in black armor.

Key words: Change, ending, new beginnings.

Meaning:

⊙ *One phase of life is closing while another begins.*

⊙ *Once the end is complete, you will be able to move on to a new beginning, and leave behind the past.*

⊙ *There is a focus on endings and beginnings, both good and bad.*

Bullet meaning: Clear away your past negativity and concentrate on a positive new beginning.

Reverse meaning: Loss, endings, failure, illness.

TEMPERANCE

14

Element: FIRE
Sign: SAGITTARIUS

THE DEVIL

15

Element: EARTH
Sign: CAPICORN

Description: A colorfully robed and winged angel stands and pours water from a cup in one hand to a cup in the other hand.

Key words: Balanced personality, tactfulness.

Meaning:

ⓖ *Patience, self-healing, self-control, and self-development.*

ⓖ *This card represents a mature and balanced personality, able to handle a situation with tact.*

ⓖ *This card may mean that you need to live frugally and manage your affairs carefully for a time.*

ⓖ *Moderation in all things.*

Bullet meaning: Learn from your past mistakes and avoid making them again.

Reverse meaning: Repeatedly making the same mistakes. Lack of self-control, uncertainty. Dispute and arguments.

Description: Baphomet or the Devil, a winged and horned creature. Below him two lesser Devils are chained to his pedestal.

Key words: Anger, oppression, restriction.

Meaning:

ⓖ *Don't dwell on negative aspects, inadequacies, or fears. Signifies unpleasant circumstances, or dark, depressing situations.*

ⓖ *There may be anger and resentment.*

ⓖ *Reflect on the present situation and ask others for advice. Move toward solving problems slowly.*

Bullet meaning: You are letting your fears hold you back.

Reverse meaning: Circumstances are negative and pessimistic. Signifies an intolerable situation, escape. Blindness and lack of perception may cause you harm.

THE TOWER

16

Element: FIRE
Planet: MARS

THE STAR

17

Element: WATER
Sign: AQUARIUS

Description: A tower is hit by lightning blowing the crown-like top away. As it falls apart, the occupants are flung to the ground.

Key words: Shocking events, accidents, revelations.

Meaning:

◎ *Destructive influences could create chaos. An accident, or a shocking or disturbing event may be on the cards.*

◎ *The card represents misery and destruction, complete and sudden change, and separations.*

◎ *Seek advice and help to get through the coming event.*

◎ *Do not lose heart, you may be able to rebuild things in a positive way.*

Bullet meaning: Ensure your life has stronger foundations. Rebuild your life.

Reverse meaning: Loss, insecurity, violence. Preventable misfortune.

Description: A naked girl kneels by a stream. She pours water on to the earth and back into the stream. Stars glow in the sky above her, and trees surround her.

Key words: Peace, relaxation, and healing.

Meaning:

◎ *This card signifies hope, faith, and harmony.*

◎ *Inspiration, refreshment, and renewal are proposed.*

◎ *There is a focus to what lies ahead, that is likely to be positive. A promise of good fortune.*

◎ *You may experience independence and inner strength.*

Bullet meaning: A bright future, tranquility, and peace.

Reverse meaning: Loss of purpose, a sense of sadness.

THE MOON

18

Element: WATER
Planet: PISCES

THE SUN

19

Element: NONE
Planet: SUN

Description: The Moon is shining brightly in the sky. A dog and a wolf stand on either side of a road, that leads between two towers. In the foreground, a lobster emerges from a dark pool.

Key words: Confusion, depression, deception. Inability to see a situation for what it is.

Meaning:

☺ *The unexpected may occur because you are spending too much time daydreaming and are not aware of reality.*

☺ *There is a focus on inner voices and intuition.*

☺ *Be wary, there is a danger or threat from something unknown.*

Bullet meaning: Keep your feet firmly on the ground. Don't allow your imagination to run away with you.

Reverse meaning: Obsession, addiction, fear, and phobias.

Description: A blazing sun shines above two children who are playing in a walled garden.

Key words: Success, optimism, and high ideas.

Meaning:

☺ *This card signifies smooth running of situations, inspiration, and purpose. You have the energy and strength to achieve great things and important desires.*

☺ *This card means ultimate success and prosperity.*

☺ *You should be content with your life, for you should have material happiness, contentment, and a successful union.*

Bullet meaning: Happiness and achievement in all areas.

Reverse meaning: Overbearing, loss of purpose.

JUDGMENT

20

Element: FIRE
Planet: PLUTO

THE WORLD

21

Element: NONE
Planet: SATURN

Description: A family rises out from the earth toward heaven. Darkness becomes light. An angel blows a trumpet above them.

Key words: Assessment, satisfying outcome.

Meaning:

⊚ *Transformation and rebirth. An end to suffering.*

⊚ *Deal with matters now that have been put to one side in order to get ahead.*

⊚ *There will be significant change, probably in the form of a new home, new relationship, new career, or perhaps a new baby.*

Bullet meaning: The start of a new era or age. The card symbolizes regeneration and a new beginning.

Reverse meaning: Self-righteous, with a narrow view of life. Regret, remorse.

Description: The World is represented by a beautiful woman dancing holding a wand in each hand; she is surrounded by a wreath and in the four corners are a winged man, an eagle, a bull and a lion.

Key words: Completion, holism, freedom.

Meaning:

⊚ *Success, achievement, and the opportunity to become aware.*

⊚ *There is a wholeness of the psyche and a feeling of completion.*

⊚ *There will be significant change in your life, but you will have completed your inner journey and you will be assured success and achievement.*

Bullet meaning: Self-confidence will bring success.

Reverse meaning: Poor self-esteem, bitter, pessimistic, and graceless emotions.

THE MINOR ARCANA

Correlating to a modern deck of playing cards, the Minor Arcana comprise 56 cards, divided into four suits: Swords, Wands, Cups, and Coins.

THE CARDS

A standard pack of cards can be substituted for the Minor Arcana, for divination purposes. Replace:

Swords	*for Spades*
Wands	*for Clubs*
Cups	*for Hearts*
Coins	*for Diamonds*

Similarly, each suit within the Minor Arcana has 10 numbered cards, from Ace to 10, together with four court cards.

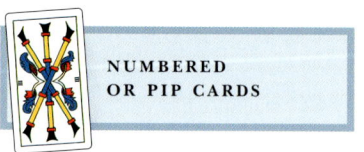

NUMBERED OR PIP CARDS

The 40 numbered cards are called pip cards, because they are usually printed with the correct number of suit symbols, or "pips." The pip cards represent ordinary events in the querent's life, and personal feelings about them. The Major Arcana, by contrast, represent events beyond our control.

COURT CARDS

The four remaining cards of each suit are called court cards – usually Page, Knight, Queen, and King. Court cards are believed to represent particular individuals, either the querent, people known to the querent, or people who will feature in the future. The elements associated with the suits will be considered when reading the court cards.

Kings, knights, and pages usually represent men; queens represent women.

King	*masculine, powerful leaders*
Queen	*feminine, powerful but more subtle and sensitive*
Knight	*masculine and skilled; progress and energy*
Page	*masculine, youthful, and lacking in wisdom*

SWORDS

Swords represent the air element. This suit is masculine and extrovert, and it reflects our state of mind, ideas, and modes of expression. Swords signify communication, arguments, and conflict. Their coloring is dark hair and green or gray eyes (*see page 19*).

Element: Air

Associated with: Gemini, Libra, Aquarius

COINS

Coins, or pentacles, represent the earth element. The suit is feminine and introvert. Coins signify wealth and the security it brings. Coins are business-minded, practical, and reliable. They may also be prudish,

wasteful, and lacking spirituality. Their coloring is dark hair and eyes (*see pages 19–20*).

Element: Earth

Associated with: Taurus, Virgo, Capricorn

WANDS

Wands represent the fire element. The suit is masculine and extrovert. Wands reflect power and energy. They see potential in a situation. They can, however, cause wanton destruction when lacking mental or physical stimulation. Their coloring is fair or auburn hair and blue eyes (*see page 19*).

Element: Fire

Associated with: Aries, Leo, Sagittarius

CUPS

Cups represent the water element. They are feminine and introvert, reflecting emotions and love for others. Cups signify sensitivity, but can also mean selfishness and manipulative behavior. Their coloring is light brown hair and gray or blue eyes (*see page 19*).

Element: Water

Associated with: Cancer, Scorpio, Pisces

SWORDS

ACE OF SWORDS

Description: A hand holds a sword aloft, around which is a victory wreath.
Meaning: Card of victory; you have won through your own hard work and effort. A stressful situation may have been resolved.
Upright meaning: Intellect, reason.
Reverse: Injustice, frustration.
Consider: You will be successful as long as you balance your emotions.

TWO OF SWORDS

Description: Two decorative, crescent-shaped swords with colorful flower motifs in the center and in each corner.
Meaning: Difficulty in decision-making. You cannot see the solution, even when it is apparent.
Upright meaning: Argument, breakdown.
Reversed: Conflict, aggression.

Consider: Do not let previous disharmony affect your communication and decision-making process. Be open-minded and considerate.

THREE OF SWORDS

Description: Three swords are surrounded by flower motifs.
Meaning: Lack of communication is, and has been, the cause of great sorrow. If you don't learn to improve your skills in this area, heartbreak could become worse.
Upright meaning: Conflict, change.
Reversed: Suffering, frustration.
Consider: Do not be upset by negative events. Things will get better.

FOUR OF SWORDS

Description: Four crescent-shaped swords surround a flower with blue and yellow leaves and petals.
Meaning: The tension around you has passed. Now is the time for contemplation and rest. A change may be necessary.

Upright meaning: Recovery, renewal.
Reversed: Isolation, loneliness.
Consider: You will feel at peace , but do not isolate yourself.

FIVE OF SWORDS

Description: This card depicts four intertwined crescent-shaped swords, with a flower in each corner. A single sword lies in the center.
Meaning: A rift or fight has occurred, possibly because of a third person. Friends are not always for life.
Upright meaning: Humiliation, betrayal, defeat.
Reversed: Dishonesty, trickery.
Consider: Beware of negative aspects of your character. Act positively, do not give in to negative feelings.

SIX OF SWORDS

Description: Six intertwined swords surround a single flower stalk.
Meaning: There is a need to escape the negative aspects around you in order to collect yourself together.

Upright meaning: Renewal, rebirth.
Reversed: Delay, postponement.
Consider: Recognize new skills and strengths, for these are the things that will have made you stronger.

SEVEN OF SWORDS

Description: On this card six intertwined crescent-shaped swords surround a single sword.
Meaning: It may be necessary to make a sacrifice that you may not want to consider. Be vigilant about health and security.
Upright meaning: Intelligence, unorthodoxy.
Reversed: Timidity, conservation, fear.
Consider: Do not blame others for your failure. Do not act hastily.

EIGHT OF SWORDS

Description: A single blue flower amid eight intertwined crescent-shaped swords.
Meaning: Feelings of frustration may

be overwhelming. It is better to wait patiently for a change in your circumstances rather than battle through, causing yourself more hurt.

Upright meaning: Delay, blockages, obstruction.

Reversed: Helplessness, feelings of frustration.

Consider: You may feel trapped. Use this time to find a solution, and plan for the future. You will then feel a new sense of determination and strength.

NINE OF SWORDS

Description: On this card eight intertwined, crescent-shaped swords surround a single sword.

Meaning: Feelings of isolation and sadness are made worse by not communicating, and always shutting others out. Past problems may be healed if they can be talked through.

Upright meaning: Anxiety, worry, suspicion.

Reversed: Depression, isolation, sadness.

Consider: Your depression will soon lift and you will become happy once again.

TEN OF SWORDS

Description: Two swords are pointing downward alongside eight intertwined, crescent-shaped swords.

Meaning: The changes occurring, that seem traumatic now, will help you to develop, allowing you to cope with other stresses in life.

Upright meaning: Caution, progress.

Reversed: Conflict, difficulty.

Consider: This card represents the end of a negative situation and the beginning of change.

PAGE OF SWORDS

Description: A youth is pictured, holding a sword aloft.

Meaning: Youthful naïveté means you are likely to run headlong into situations. Don't rush to fight for others without all the facts.

Upright meaning: Caution, tact, diplomacy, wariness.

Reversed: Mistrust, suspicion.

Consider: Secretiveness can lead to confusion and lack of trust.

KNIGHT OF SWORDS

Description: A knight in armor on a steed is depicted with his sword in his left hand thrust up into the air. He is galloping away from the battle scene.

Meaning: Someone often involved in conflict. They may be clever and skilled; however, their talents may be better used in negotiating rather than fighting.

Upright meaning: Courage, conviction, strength.

Reversed: Aggression, impatience.

Consider: Beware of acting impulsively or erratically. Seek to create balance.

QUEEN OF SWORDS

Description: A queen is pictured seated upon a throne and holding her sword upright.

Meaning: A lively but impulsive person. A queen can be impatient and may cause conflict due to her restless nature.

Upright meaning: Independence, ambition, drive to succeed.

Reversed: Loneliness, coldness, and aloofness.

Consider: Highlight the positive aspects in your life, and be aware of the potential that the future holds. Respect and acknowledge the pain of others.

KING OF SWORDS

Description: A robed king is pictured seated and holding a staff upright in his right hand.

Meaning: A fair-minded person who knows their own mind. You may cause conflict because of your insensitivity and lack of regard for the feelings of others.

Upright meaning: Authority, power, innovation.

Reversed: Cruelty, malice, and exploitation.

Consider: Make sure that you do not become bitter or cold-hearted. You are, or will be, involved with someone who is determined and rather detached.

WANDS

ACE OF WANDS

Description: A hand thrusts a bright green branch surrounded by colorful leaves out of a glowing sun.

Meaning: This is the initiation of energy. You are enthusiastic about a plan or event and want to get it started.

Upright meaning: Creativity, energy, ambition.

Reversed: Frustration, apathy, lack of interest, or feeling.

Consider: This is a powerful card that signifies new opportunities.

TWO OF WANDS

Description: Two colorful crossed wands surrounded by flower motifs.

Meaning: There are lots of talks and discussions. There may be a lot of advice being given to try and influence you. Teaching is also aspected. There may be a focus on your relationship with others. There is frequently a need for independence and solitude.

Upright meaning: Assessment, planning, decision.

Reversed: Self-doubt, anti-climax, a sense of conflict.

Consider: Assert your own independence and don't allow others to sway you. Be strong.

THREE OF WANDS

Description: On this card four red and blue leaves are placed alongside three crossed red, blue, yellow, and black wands.

Meaning: Those around you are watching you; they are likely to copy your actions. You are unaware that you are being observed. Be a leader, not a follower.

Upright meaning: Beginnings, optimism, luck.

Reversed: A tendency to delay, indecision, procrastination.

Consider: Try to maintain an optimistic outlook, but concentrate on realistic goals in life or you will be disappointed when you fail to attain them.

FOUR OF WANDS

Description: Four intertwined, colorful wands are crossed and surrounded by flowers.

Meaning: Your dreams are more accessible if you are able to put aside self-interest and work with others. Work as a team; the whole is always greater than the sum of its parts.

Upright meaning: Creativity, openness, adventure.

Reversed: Frustration, resentment.

Consider: Enjoy this period, that will be harmonious and positive.

SIX OF WANDS

Description: Six colorful, intertwined wands are crossed, with a flower above and below.

Meaning: You have beaten the opposition. Now it is necessary to carry on; it may be that you will need to take a closer look at your life, or even reconstruct parts of your life.

Upright meaning: Good fortune, reward, satisfaction.

Reversed: Setbacks, conflict.

Consider: Offer friendship to old foes and repair old relationships.

FIVE OF WANDS

Description: Four intertwined wands with a single wand in the center.

Meaning: You are up against strong competitors. Fight through with determination and you will win.

Upright meaning: Challenge, growth.

Reversed: Setbacks, argument.

Consider: Be honest with yourself about goals, aspirations, and needs, so you can realize your desires.

SEVEN OF WANDS

Description: Six intertwined, crossed wands with a single wand in the center and flowers either side.

Meaning: Don't allow others to destroy everything you have worked for so long to achieve. Think of a plan of action. Your feelings and beliefs may also be under threat.

Upright meaning: Effort, success, achievement, fulfillment.

Reversed: Failure, self-doubt.
Consider: Concentrate on internal and external challenges. Be prepared to make changes.

EIGHT OF WANDS

Description: Eight intertwined wands with a yellow flower above and below.
Meaning: Suddenly the speed of your life has increased in all directions. You have several opportunities of which you can make use.
Upright meaning: Progress, completion, fulfillment.
Reversed: Confusion, misdirection.
Consider: Know your desires and take the initiative to realize them.

NINE OF WANDS

Description: A single wand in the center of eight intertwined wands
Meaning: Setbacks have left you feeling you have been let down. Don't let past problems make you so guarded. Allow others to help you.
Upright meaning: Resilience, reward.

Reversed: Reluctance, setbacks, failure, conflict.
Consider: Do not lose faith. Be strong and you will be rewarded.

TEN OF WANDS

Description: Two wands in the center of eight intertwined wands.
Meaning: Let other people look after their own responsibilities. If you carry everyone else's burdens, you will have no time to see to your own.
Upright meaning: Responsibility, commitment.
Reversed: Exhaustion, confusion.
Consider: Try to be more generous with your time and your money and you will regain inner peace.

PAGE OF WANDS

Description: On this card a page is depicted proudly holding a bright green branch.
Meaning: You desire to know more about the world, and perhaps learn through study or travel.

Upright meaning: Energy, vigor, new beginnings.

Reversed: Apathy, mistrust, suspicion.

Consider: A close friend may help to enlighten you.

KNIGHT OF WANDS

Description: A knight in a wide brimmed hat clutches his branch as he rides an anarchic horse.

Meaning: A very dynamic person, skilled and enthusiastic. You may have an excessive personality that could lead to imbalance of your resources or energy.

Upright meaning: Excitement, unpredictability.

Reversed: Stress, impatience, recklessness, lack of caution.

Consider: Your goals are soon to be realized. Have faith.

QUEEN OF WANDS

Description: A fair-haired queen is pictured with her wand, like a scepter, in one hand.

Meaning: A Queen of Wands is a friendly, often supportive person, who is independent and single-minded. There is also the possibility of further education or travel.

Upright meaning: Energy, ability, a sense of purpose.

Reversed: Interference, arrogance.

Consider: Seek advice during this time of spiritual development.

KING OF WANDS

Description: A colorfully robed king with a wide brimmed crown is pictured with his wand that he holds like a scepter.

Meaning: An ambitious man, who does nothing by halves. There is a need to be more disciplined, or the King of Wands runs the risk of being foolhardy or reckless.

Upright meaning: Intelligence, generosity, magnanimity.

Reversed: Intolerance, foolhardiness, narrow-mindedness.

Consider: You should be feeling confident; this can be used to inspire others whose situation is not as stable as yours.

COINS

ACE OF COINS

Description: A large, beautifully decorated golden coin is encircled by colorful flower motifs.

Meaning: There is a doorway opening for you now or in the near future; it is likely to mean business or work opportunities.

Upright meaning: Stability, security, contentment.

Reversed: Instability, anxiety.

Consider: This is a positive time, but beware of being carried away by material wealth.

TWO OF COINS

Description: A decorative S-shape surrounds two golden coins.

Meaning: There is a great deal going on in your life; you are juggling several aspects at once. You may need to be more flexible to fit everything in. A career move is possible.

Upright meaning: A sense of contentment, optimism.

Reversed: Impatience, recklessness.

Consider: Keep your affairs balanced, for there will be a great many rewards.

THREE OF COINS

Description: A trail of blue and red flowers are entwined around three golden coins.

Meaning: The learning of a new skill or beginning of study. Recognize the fact that you may not always know everything. Learn from others.

Upright meaning: Reward, recompense, satisfaction.

Reversed: Frustration, criticism.

Consider: You will get personal satisfaction from a venture, and receive spiritual rewards.

FOUR OF COINS

Description: Four golden coins, surrounded by blue and red flowers encircle a colorful shield.

Meaning: A need to get money together for an unforeseen expense. Worries over finances are possible.

Upright meaning: Security, stability, predictability.

Reversed: Reluctance, resistance.

Consider: You will be rewarded financially, but in order to get there, you may suffer a loss, such as a death, or the end of a job.

FIVE OF COINS

Description: Five golden coins decorated with flower motifs are surrounded by red and blue flowers and leaves. Either side is the Roman numeral for five.

Meaning: This is a warning. You need to make time for certain aspects of your life before things start to deteriorate further. Take care of health and financial matters.

Upright meaning: Difficulty, uncertainty, insecurity.

Reversed: Isolation, helplessness.

Consider: Look at your situation to decide whether or not there is a solution. Take care not to become involved in something that is bound to end in loss.

SIX OF COINS

Description: A four-pointed red and blue flower is surrounded by six golden coins.

Meaning: You may be giving too much time and money to others, who may not be the ideal focus of your energies. You must care for yourself and family as well.

Upright meaning: Fairness, generosity.

Reversed: Unhappiness, carelessness.

Consider: You may find yourself in a rewarding or influential position. Be generous.

SEVEN OF COINS

Description: Four golden coins in each corner with three at the center surrounded by red and blue leaves.

Meaning: A time to reap the rewards of hard work. The results may seem small compared to the labor expended. You may also experience anxiety over money.

Upright meaning: Perseverance, effort, luck.
Reversed: Defeat, acceptance.
Consider: Use enthusiasm and hard work to get profit. Lack of vision will mean failure.

EIGHT OF COINS

Description: Four golden coins in the center are surrounded by four larger coins.
Meaning: You carry things out with care and precision. Through experience you have become skilled in your work. You are a hard worker.
Upright meaning: Progress, prosperity, pride.
Reversed: Defeat, acceptance.
Consider: Do not lose interest in areas of your life outside your work. They are important too.

NINE OF COINS

Description: Eight golden coins, with one coin in the center, encircled by an elaborate flower pattern.

Meaning: There is a wish to be recognized for your achievements.
Upright meaning: Achievement, security, solitude.
Reversed: Insecurity, dependency.
Consider: Financial rewards will bring pleasure. You will experience new self-worth.

TEN OF COINS

Description: Ten golden coins are divided by a red and blue flower.
Meaning: Stable financial and material aspects. Joint finance is an important area.
Upright meaning: Security, support.
Reversed: Interference, hindrance.
Consider: Now is the opportunity to repay people for past kindnesses. Share your wealth and rewards.

PAGE OF COINS

Description: A young man holds a coin, and looks wistfully ahead.
Meaning: Look for new and challenging areas in your life. Take on

more responsibility for a more material reward.

Upright meaning: Dependability, reliability, security.

Reversed: Frustration, unhappiness.

Consider: You will be rewarded for self-discipline and determination.

KNIGHT OF COINS

Description: A knight on horseback gazes at a coin in the sky.

Meaning: A man keen on developing his work potential. This is a time of particular energy and hard work. If he is negative, this man may have little direction.

Upright meaning: Practicality, dependability.

Reversed: Stagnation, boredom.

Consider: Appreciate the help and work of others – in particular a man who may be very loyal.

QUEEN OF COINS

Description: A queen in colorful robes is depicted holding a coin aloft in her right hand, in her left hand is a scepter.

Meaning: A woman wishing to increase her potential in the work field. There needs to be a little more balance and harmony in other areas of her life.

Upright meaning: Openness, sensitivity, generosity.

Reversed: Stagnation, boredom.

Consider: Be thankful for a good situation, and do not lose confidence in yourself.

KING OF COINS

Description: A king in a wide brimmed hat is pictured with a coin in one hand. He is seated on a throne with his legs crossed.

Meaning: A powerful man economically. Confidence in the work situation ensures people don't think of him as being overconfident.

Upright meaning: Honesty, practicality, security.

Reversed: Greed, weakness.

Consider: Show respect for someone who is intelligent about business matters, but recognize that he may have an empty spiritual life.

CUPS

ACE OF CUPS

Description: A large, elaborate chalice in the shape of a castle.
Meaning: This is a time for emotional fulfillment. There is a feeling of joy and contentment, both spiritually and emotionally. Fertility is also aspected.
Upright meaning: Love, contentment, emotion, growth.
Reversed: Sadness, loneliness, disappointment.
Consider: This is a good time to explore new experiences, that should be successful.

TWO OF CUPS

Description: Two golden cups stand alongside a pedestal of flowers.
Meaning: There may be new depth to your relationship, or the beginning of a new one.
Upright meaning: Support, trust.

Reversed: Betrayal, separation.
Consider: You may find love with someone you had never considered before. Keep your mind open!

THREE OF CUPS

Description: Three golden cups are intertwined by blue and red flowers.
Meaning: This is a time to enjoy life, to go out with friends and celebrate.
Upright meaning: Optimism, growth.
Reversed: Selfishness, exploitation.
Consider: Clear the air of difficult relationships and try to establish new ground for a friendship.

FOUR OF CUPS

Description: An elaborate, colorful branch with red and blue leaves is surrounded by four golden cups.
Meaning: There may be an offer of friendship. You might not realize that this person would be a beneficial influence, since he or she would not normally interest you. Take a risk and trust them.

Upright meaning: Boredom, apathy.
Reversed: Self-pity, indulgence.
Consider: Do not give in to anxieties or difficulties. The future is positive and bright.

FIVE OF CUPS

Description: One golden cup in the center with four golden cups in each corner. Between the cups grow red, yellow, and blue flowers.
Meaning: Past sorrow and disillusionment are preventing you from forming new relationships. Try to face the future and don't dwell on what has been.
Upright meaning: Unhappiness, regret, loss.
Reversed: Remorse, sadness.
Consider: Consider your reasons for negative feelings and try to establish a positive goal.

SIX OF CUPS

Description: Six upright golden cups stand alongside a decorative baton made up of colorful flower motifs.
Meaning: It is important to examine and develop your emotional communication. You need to learn how to build on what you already have, and to give and receive on an emotional level.
Upright meaning: Reminiscing, rewards.
Reversed: Nostalgia, delay.
Consider: You will feel peaceful. Look at the world around you and take pleasure in noticing or doing simple things.

SEVEN OF CUPS

Description: On this card six golden cups are depicted above and below a larger golden cup in the center, surrounded by flower motifs.
Meaning: You are confused with dreams, plans, and wishes. Decide first what you most want out of life, then pursue it.
Upright meaning: Illusion, choice.
Reversed: Delusion, fantasy.
Consider: Do not panic about delays and setbacks; use this valuable time to reflect on the positive things in your life.

EIGHT OF CUPS

Description: Six golden cups above and below two golden cups in the center of the card.

Meaning: You are looking for a deeper meaning to your life; you need to pursue this to feel content.

Upright meaning: Development, sacrifice, growth.

Reversed: Uncertainty, change.

Consider: When you have decided upon your pursuit, you will be able to seek happiness and fulfillment.

NINE OF CUPS

Description: Nine golden cups are intertwined with red and blue flowers.

Meaning: You should be pleased with all you have achieved in your life so far. Now is the time to enjoy the fruits of your success.

Upright meaning: Happiness, optimism, generosity.

Reversed: Complacency, smugness, superficiality.

Consider: Make the most of this positive time and use your own good fortune to help others.

TEN OF CUPS

Description: Nine golden cups stand upright in rows of three, above them is a larger golden cup lying on its side.

Meaning: A time of emotional commitments. Look at the type of relationships you form.

Upright meaning: Fulfillment, contentment.

Reversed: Disruption, unhappiness.

Consider: This is a strong, positive card. Use this very beneficial time to help those around you.

PAGE OF CUPS

Description: A page is pictured with a covered golden cup.

Meaning: A young man finds out more about life from meetings and friendships with others, both professionally and socially.

Upright meaning: Sensitivity, modesty.

Reversed: Dissatisfaction, apathy.

Consider: Beware of accepting proposals too easily. Assess what you really want before making changes. The time may not be right.

KNIGHT OF CUPS

Description: A knight appears on horseback, holding a cup.

Meaning: This may represent a man that the querent may be emotionally involved with. It is a positive time to show others how you feel toward them.

Upright meaning: Idealism, originality, optimism.

Reversed: Deception, concealment.

Consider: Use your imagination; there may be an invitation to which you will respond with excitement.

QUEEN OF CUPS

Description: A fair-haired queen appears holding a large cup, with a thin white rod in her left hand.

Meaning: A kind, friendly woman, she may be a person with whom the querent is emotionally involved. The card also denotes great spirituality.

Upright meaning: Sensitivity, kindness.

Reversed: Vanity, selfishness.

Consider: A positive time; make use of it to strengthen your relationships with others.

KING OF CUPS

Description: A king with a wide brimmed crown appears holding a golden cup.

Meaning: An emotionally secure man, he is able to give and receive love on many levels. If negative, he may become indolent, idle, and self-indulgent.

Upright meaning: Sophistication, coldness.

Reversed: Deception, manipulation.

Consider: Your actions may revolve around emotions, and you may come across a person who stimulates your spiritual development.

TAROT ETIQUETTE

When people consult a card-reader, palmist, or other person with divinatory skills, they may want help with a problem. Divination may, under those circumstances, become a type of counseling, and counseling of any kind involves responsibility. All information you discuss should remain confidential.

Be constructive – never negative – when giving advice. If you feel out of your depth, be honest, and recommend a professional counselor or a more experienced reader.

FURTHER READING

ANDERSON, W., *Fortune-Telling* (Parragon, 1995)

DONALDSON, T., *Step-by-Step Tarot* (Thorsons, 1996)

KAPLAN, Stuart J., *Encyclopedia of the Tarot* (US Games Systems Inc., 1978, 1985, 1986)

KNIGHT, Gareth, *The Treasure House of Images* (Aquarian, 1986)

MANN, A. T., *The Tarot* (Element, 1989)

POLLACK, Rachel, *The New Tarot* (Aquarian, 1989)

WAITE, A.E., *The Pictorial Key to Tarot* (Parragon, 1986)

TAROT CARD DECKS

Traditional Decks
Tarot de Marseilles
Rider-Waite Tarot deck

More Recent Decks
Arthurian Tarot, John and Caitlin Matthews; illustrated by Miranda Grey

Australian Contemporary Dreamtime Tarot, Keith and Daicon Courtney-Peto

The Celtic Tarot, Courtney Davis

Enochian Tarot, Gerald and Betty Schueler; painted by Sallie Ann Glassman

Jungian Tarot, Robert Wang

Magical Tarot Deck, designed by Anthony Clark

Motherpeace Tarot, Vicki Noble

The Mythic Tarot, Juliet Sharman-Burke and Liz Greene; illustrated by Tricia Newell

Native American Tarot, Magda and J. A. Gonzalez

Servants of the Light, designed by Jo Gill, Dolores Ashcroft-Nowicki and Anthony Clark

The Shining Woman Tarot, Rachel Pollack

Xultun Maya Tarot, Peter Balin

INDEX

*Other titles in the
Pocket Prophecy
series are:*

NUMEROLOGY

PALMISTRY

RUNES